EVERYDAY JUSTICE

Amorphous Publishing Guild
Buffalo, NY USA
First Printing, 2025
www.Amorphous.Press

EVERYDAY JUSTICE

KEN JP STUCZYNSKI

AmorphousPublishingGuild

To my daughter Christina,
an inspiration,
a hope for the future,
and another reason for me to be good.

CONTENTS

Foreword: A Confession

If I am to be completely honest, there's something you ought to know. As much as you may need this book, I needed to write it for my own sake — to exorcise my demons. I have always found myself angry at injustice, and there's a lot of injustice in the world. More than one friend suggests that's a common trait of autism, something I would perhaps have been diagnosed with had I been born a decade or two later. Regardless of labels, I think a lot of us feel what I'm talking about.

However, I have to take responsibility for how I deal with it. I am ashamed of how unkind I am at times on social media. Not with friends and acquaintances, mind you, but behind the quasi-anonymity of blowing off steam in comment sections full of strangers. And then there are pet peeves. I almost started a website for shaming people who park badly. I flirted with the idea of fake parking citations, and even more questionable forms of "street justice" to inconvenience those who inconvenience others. This is not how I want to think of myself. This is not who I want to be, or be remembered.

Mind you, I don't think this means forfeiting my voice. It still feels wrong to remain silent on important issues, or not take action to protect others. But so much is beyond my control, and there's so little benefit to gripe about everything, everywhere, all the time. Sometimes I have to set boundaries in my own life. Wearing every bit of my heart on my sleeve risks making topics of annoyance my identity.

I regularly doom-scroll, an unhealthy habit given social media is full of outrage-bait. It's hard not to be exposed to a deluge of disturbing news, both real and fabricated. The more I am aware of what is going on in the world, the more I have to consciously decide either to be upset or struggle for some positive perspective. Ideally, I can focus on the things I talk about in this book, as it is heavily based on personal experience. In the worst times, I brace for some inevitable wreck, watching a collision in slow motion, helplessly paralyzed as if in a dream. As a historian of sorts and a follower of geopolitics, I've found some wrecks accurately predicted in the end. But did pulling the fire alarm in posts and my intellectual blog make a difference?

It's all too easy to just yell at the world. And there is sometimes little difference between a grumpy pessimist, an apathetic nihilist, and a cold realist. The point is that the grumpy, apathetic, and cold parts are optional. And as we can learn from people like Dr. Martin Luther King, Jr., pessimism and hope are not opposites, nor are they incompatible. Belief in the long arc of history bending toward justice may be a matter of faith. To believe such may be unrealistic or even unreasonable, but maybe the belief we choose determines the outcome more than the other way around, at least in our own lives.

So let's assume I can't solve any of the world's problems, or stop injustice like some superhero or messianic activist. How can I make peace with my imperfect self and an imperfect world? What personal value do I bring to the immediate world around me? Do my words and actions make the world a better place, even if just a little? Am I bringing a light to others or just cursing the darkness? Am I acting as judge, jury, and executioner in the way I think about other people's actions? Could such energy be better spent fixing things and helping others instead of condemning the breakers of rules and the breachers of peace?

In recent years, I've discovered a sharp contrast at times between doing what is "just" and doing what is "right". A message from the

Galilee of a hundred generations ago was clear — even though we have been told we should judge and punish, there is another way. We can repay evil with kindness. Keeping score isn't as important as mercy. Real justice isn't about enforcing and power, but standing up for the powerless and forgiving the imperfect (which is all of us, including myself). This brings us back to the question: Is it better to condemn and punish a wrong, or do something to right it?

I know the answer. I think we all do. So why don't we do something? Negative emotions take over. But even more, we lack faith. Mind you, I don't mean "faith" as believing in what we can't know, but knowing what we can't believe. We all know deep down inside what is true and good. What is hard is to accept it and act.

My hope is that the reader can tap into that faith we all share as living beings. It takes effort, even dedication, to overcome the inertia of apathy. It often takes outright courage to do the right thing. The things in this book will not generally risk one's life or safety, but by big or small actions and choices, is taking a courageous stand nonetheless. A tide may not turn in the end, but I suggest everything we do here and now matters. Logical or not, that is how I choose to live my life. What I do reflects who I am, or can even bring me closer to the person I believe I should be. I hope this book inspires the reader to feel the same way.

~ Ken

Why Shopping Carts?

S o ... why did I mention shopping carts* in the subtitle of this book?

A few years back, a meme popularized an idea that became known as "shopping cart theory". It suggests "a person's character and their ability to self-govern can be judged by whether or not they return a shopping cart to its designated area." This, of course, is judging people, which is always a two-edged sword. It may be useful and wise to note other people's actions. For example, how someone treats the wait staff at a restaurant, where intention and context aren't filled with unknowns. It's a pretty clear conclusion. Similarly, things like littering are wrong and a nuisance in any conceivable circumstance. But a shopping cart?

The assumption is that it's a simple act of civic responsibility, or courtesy toward others. My wife blew her lid once because a woman shoved her finished cart toward our car. I only held her back because I don't like confrontation and didn't think it was worth it. But her ire seemed just, since the woman apparently didn't care and was risking damage to other people's property. This is one context for one situation.

What other contexts are possible? Was the cart placed out of the way or taking up parking spaces? Was there a convenient cart corral nearby, and were they just lazy? Were there winds to increase the chances of stray collisions? There are surely different levels of inconvenience and culpability. And yet we want to judge someone by this act as a benchmark of morality. There are even "Cart Narcs" on YouTube who publicly shame people to entertain their viewership.

The other side of that two-edged sword was explored by Krystal D'Costa, who wrote a 2017 paper in Scientific American on the subject. The explanations she found for why these deeds were done (or not done, rather) included bad weather, distance from a return area, leaving children unattended, and disability. Beliefs were also involved, such as it being the job of store workers, or the convenience of others taking the cart where it was left.

But all of this is beside the point of this book. It bothers me (more than it probably should) when I see people just leave their cart about thoughtlessly (in my opinion). When I see someone finishing unloading their cart, I have a choice to make. Do I wait and watch, ready to judge? The stress of anticipation seems ridiculous when I think about it. It's not my job to police other people's levels of respect or courtesy. But it's in my immediate surroundings and I can't help thinking about it.

For some time now, this is what I do: I wait for them to be done and offer to take it from them. If I'm done shopping, I take it with mine to the corral (or store). If I'm going into the store, I take it with me as my cart, even if I don't need one. Either way, I replace a possible annoyance with friendliness and a good deed. Even if they were going to abandon it carelessly, I might have moved the needle on their sense of trust and responsibility the next time — just by being nice.

This sort of choice is what this book is about.

* *Also known as "trolleys" or "buggies" or by other names among our English-speaking friends outside the United States.*

CHAPTER 1

Be the Change

Usually attributed to Mahatma Gandhi, it was Brooklyn high school teacher Arleen Lorrance who first wrote, "Be the change you want to see in the world." This notion came after a period of looking around her school and community, finding only poverty, violence, and hopelessness. As some point, she realized that things were not going to fix themselves, and waiting for change or someone's help was unbearable. Some of us feel this way in our own communities. We either sink or swim. We give up, or decide with real conviction that we will do something. That decision is choosing a positive attitude and belief — hope.

But reality will always press against us. Can one person doing one act make a difference? Based on Loren Eiseley's essay, "The Star Thrower", a well-shared starfish story is usually told as follows:

A man was walking along a beach and there were thousands of stranded starfish that had been swept in on the tide would soon die. He noticed a man in the distance who was throwing them back into the water, one at a time. As he approached the man he exclaimed, "There are so many! You can't possibly make a difference!" The man simply threw another starfish back into the ocean and said, "I made a difference to that one..."

If you can make just one person's life a little better, even just for today, care enough to decide it's worth the trouble.

At the very least, it will make a difference for yourself. A study* shows a strong correlation between those who are "emotionally and behaviorally compassionate" and "well-being, happiness, health, and longevity". Correlation isn't causation, but I suggest our behaviors have a profound effect on who we are, not just the other way around.

We don't fully appreciate the impact we have on others and the world just by being ourselves. We want to think we matter, but don't feel like we do. We may need to be reminded. It's no wonder the story "It's a Wonderful Life" has been reiterated in numerous television shows.

C.S. Lewis brings the impact of our actions, good and bad, to another level:

Good and evil both increase at compound interest. That is why the little decisions you and I make every day are of such infinite importance. The smallest good act today is the capture of a strategic point from which, a few months later, you may be able to go on to victories you never dreamed of. An apparently trivial indulgence in lust or anger today is the loss of a ridge or railway line or bridgehead from which the enemy may launch an attack otherwise impossible.

Not all of us can start a charity or organize an event to increase good works. However, as you will see throughout this book, there are countless opportunities for making a difference. In Hinduism, one of the Paths to the Divine is Karma Yoga — the way of service. In Judaism, we have Mitzvahs (a word that means good deeds but imperative enough to be "commandments"). In Islam, good deeds are essential to fulfill religious duty. And we have the universal Golden Rule of "do unto others ..."

In Scouting, a good deed is called a "Good Turn" — seeking out people and situations in need and taking the initiative to assist. Helping the old lady across the street comes to mind, but it could be asking if someone is lost and giving directions, or picking up litter, or doing any number of other things mentioned in this book.

The commonality is that when something needs to be done, we don't shake our fist or get angry about it. We step up and do it. We take responsibility even when we could argue that it's someone else's. Again, shopping carts being put back is a perfect example. We can't personally change every one else's behavior any more than the weather, so why not just set it right when we can?

And when more and more people catch on to such a solution, the world itself may be changed. As Desmond Tutu instructs us, "Do your little bit of good where you are; it's those little bits of good put together that overwhelm the world."

*Int. J. Behav. Med. 12, 66–77 (2005). https://doi.org/10.1207/s15327558ijbm1202_4

CHAPTER 2

Begin at Home

The saying "Charity begins at home" was never meant to be an either-or proposition as some people make it. But it's easy to neglect those you love (and count on you) when busy helping the less fortunate. There are times I jumped at helping a friend a few times too often, while things around the house didn't get done. It's about "work-life-service" balance.

There's an expression in Freemasonry to "do your best in that which lies nearest to you". Simply put, we have more influence over things near than far — and therefore more ability and responsibility. Sure, we can outsource our help using dollars to aid victims of a tsunami or nuclear disaster half the world away. And sometimes we can provide more help in dollars because we make enough money to support more work by others than we could do with our own time. Regardless of such ability to extend good works afar, your very self and home can be a foundation for bringing light to the world.

Before we go anywhere with this, it must be said: Self-care is not optional. We need time and a place to recharge ourselves. We could even say that it's harder, or even impossible, to love others if we don't love ourselves. I shouldn't be the one to cast the first stone on this one, but take care of yourself first when you can.* Think of the instructions for those breathing masks on airplanes.

Something was lovingly brought to my attention not long ago that shook me. When I am regularly, outwardly upset about current affairs in the world, it takes away the ability for visitors – and even family – to find sanctuary in my home. Yes, the word used was sanctuary — a place of calm in the storm. I have never thought of it that way. I also learned that people looked to my company for peace and solace. I never thought of myself as a refuge for others, but they thought that of me.

Talk about a mighty responsibility! Talk about being the change in the world! Just being there for people, especially when it's tough not to be upset, is a huge act of kindness.

Making your home welcoming may mean very different things to different people, but it's something that deserves serious consideration. The concept of home is a safe, personal space, one that affects our lives perhaps more than anything other thing or condition.

There are also things you can do that are much larger commitments. Adopting or fostering a child is life-changing for everyone involved. Adopting (rescuing) or fostering a pet can be just as meaningful for some people. Choosing a child with special needs, or an injured pet, is an even greater responsibility. We live in a world of wars, natural disasters, abandoned and neglected people and animals.

And it can be an act of righteous defiance. When I found out the stray kitten in our bushes was tossed out a window a few houses down, I was furious. The man who did it even tore down the signs I initially put up about the lost pet, and told their children it wasn't the one that went missing! It was my kitten now, part of MY family. Deciding to Love – because someone else refused to – feels like conquering the evils of the world, replacing selfishness, injustice, and apathy with decisive, unconditional Love.

Sometimes it can't be you that saves a child or pet. You may be the facilitator, or support those who can. Remember, to help instead of potentially make things worse, be sure you and your family have the personal strength and resources to welcome others into your home. And be sure not to use such things with the expectation to "fix" or "fill a hole" in your life — even though in some way it probably will.

For those into psychology, consider Maslow's Hierarchy of Needs.

CHAPTER 3

The Neighborhood

Things close to our home also affect us more than we realize, such as the condition of our neighborhood. Good deeds here improve everyone's quality of life. Taking care of our own sidewalk may be required by law, but doing a good job removing snow or fixing it may save someone from injury. If you have a lawn mower or snow blower, why not also hit the neighbor's lot since you are out? Maybe they don't have the equipment and a little work on your part saves a lot on theirs. Maybe they don't have the time, or are infirmed. Or maybe you are just building goodwill and trust, and they may return the favor. But even if they don't, you can take pride in taking the step.

Get to know your neighbors. You may find the reason they do (or don't do) some things is a disability or other circumstance. Maybe they park differently due to accessibility issues. Maybe we need to be a bit quieter during the day for that sleeping neighbor who works third shift.

Maybe there's a shut-in you should keep an eye on. Nothing is more heartbreaking than someone who fell and wasn't found for days. (That's an extreme but very possible scenario. In fact, it happened to a relative of ours.) Don't assume everyone has "someone else," like family or associates, to ensure their well-being.

If there is a block club, join it. Sometimes that's the only way to get to know your neighbors. If there isn't one, find out if there is interest and start one. Block club or not, report suspicious activity. Let someone know they forgot about alternate parking so they don't get a ticket.

Maybe you have a little space where people walk by. Flowers and decorations can bring a smile to people's faces. Maybe you can do even more. A place to sit, a shelter from the rain — it all depends on the space that is yours to use. How about setting out a "Little Library" where people can take or donate old books? (See LittleFreeLibrary.Org.) Near my home, people started hanging bags with gloves and hats from trees in the wintertime for those who needed it.

There's no end to the possibilities of making available simple things that can improve people's quality of life. May daughter recently lent me the book, "The Serviceberry: Abundance and Reciprocity in the Natural World" by Robin Wall Kimmerer. It's all about openly sharing without keeping score, rather than seeing everything we do as transactional. That's a sort of economic model I've always tried to establish between people I know. Knowing I was reading the book motivated my wife to buy me a Serviceberry sapling, which I hope to become an abundant source of berries for any passerby who wishes a treat. Imagine if every house had a fruit tree of some kind that anyone could take from. It's very foreign to the way we usually do things, but maybe it's time for a better way, one front yard at a time.

Not all ideas are intuitive or obvious. Too many strays? Contact a program that spays and neuters stray cats and then releases them back into the neighborhood. This keeps the rodent population down, while keeping out more strays that are not vaccinated or safe.

Even symbolic things matter. I have a "Peace Pole" in my front yard — something I saw at D'Youville College (now University) that inspired me to make one for my home. You can find them around the world. (See WorldPeace.Org.) Mine is a wooden stake with the words "May Peace Prevail On Earth" in the four languages spoken in my neighborhood — English, Spanish, Arabic, and Chinese. It's a welcoming message for all.

The most important question may be "Who is my neighbor?" Is it only the people you share a driveway with? Only citizens? Is it only people who have a home? What about the residents of a halfway house? Why draw lines at all? If they live around you, you can help them. Their need is the problem, and you have solutions, even if it's just letting them know you are there for them.

CHAPTER 4

On the Road

Why are people so rude in traffic? Why are otherwise civil people tempted toward road rage?

I have a theory. In your car, you are anonymous. You may never see other drivers again. As in a huge online discussion medium, there's less consequence in venting or being uncivil. But the flip side is that other drivers do impact your life and safety. As anonymous as they might seem, it feels personal when they do something to offend or endanger you. A vehicle may feel like a private space and others can easily disturb your peace.

Ever notice there are plenty of ways to express your displeasure to other drivers, but none to express an apology for making a mistake? It's all too easy to honk in anger or gesture in hostility. Things can even lead to physical confrontation. Often worse, it leads to accidents. But if you have the ability to do all that, you also have the ability to do the opposite. Be courteous. Be apologetic. Try not to block traffic. Make room for tractor-trailers to move over.

To be successful in this, you have to have awareness. You have to have a bit of patience, knowing that letting a car in from the side street may cost you a few seconds, but save them a minute or more. Be aware when a pedestrian needs to cross and is having trouble. Where you stop and what you block make a difference.

Make eye contact and smile. We need to recognize each other as human beings, not soulless vehicles.

Consider that not everyone driving too fast or too slow (for our taste) is being discourteous. Even if they are, they may just not be aware. It may be where they are in life, struggling with age, or a broken-down car. And if you trust in fate or a divine will, being delayed for a moment may mean avoiding an accident down the road.

As pedestrians, cyclists, and drivers, we can try to be more aware of one another. Don't assume everyone else can see you, and try not to make others feel worried about endangering you by being too close. It's all common sense when you give it conscious thought.

As passengers, we can give up our seat on public transportation to those who need it more. We can take up less space when there's little room, and let people know there is space if they seem like they are looking.

Courtesy can build and spread trust in general just as a smile can be contagious. You can make someone's day a little harder or a little easier. It's our choice —a lot of meaningful choices just getting from A to B.

CHAPTER 5

In the Marketplace

In a famous series of Zen Buddhist drawings called the "Ten Bulls", the last image depicts the newly-Enlightened person returning to "the marketplace". This refers to the everyday world of people and things — the place where we most interact with other people.. We can be calm or contemplative by ourselves, but how we act and treat other people is at the heart of all morality. It's about character, reputation, and social standing. But in a big world, like on the road, we encounter so many people in a nearly anonymous way.

The easiest thing to do is smile. It doesn't always mean to everyone as you walk by — there are places and times it isn't appropriate or the local custom. In some places, eye contact is expected; in others, it can be taken as confrontational. In some places, even making conversation with strangers is a major cultural *faux pas*. But you can go out of your way to be pleasant when you do interact.

The largest opportunity to brighten someone's day is in retail. Workers are sometimes dejected, exhausted, even abused by both customers and bosses. A sincere, caring smile can take the edge off. Making the effort not to be an undue imposition lets them breathe. And showing appreciation is golden. An innocent compliment can make their day. A compliment to their manager is the next level.

If you're attitude is that it's their job and they get paid to serve you with a smile, and you eagerly cut their tip for having a bad day, this book probably isn't for you. On the other hand, acknowledging that their work is really busy and they may be having a tough time is real empathy. Giving a bit extra (assuming it is a place where tipping is acceptable) may make up for those who were stingy.

You can also choose to shop at local businesses that may be having a hard time competing. Or you could buy "fair trade" goods made in developing nations through exchanges dedicated to raising the standard of living of our poorest populations. There are even systems where you can give microloans to help such people and families start businesses. Heifer International, for example, allows you to cover the expense of livestock, such as a goat or beehive, to help families become more self-sufficient. The whole world is a marketplace now.

At brick-and-mortar establishments, you can set the bad actions of others straight. We already talked about shopping carts. But what about people who abandon perishables in non-refrigerated areas? They are basically throwing out other people's food. If you find it, taking it to the checkout will enable them to make the decision if it is safe to put back on the shelf.

Other customers may be having a bad or sad day, and you could just let them be. Open the door for them, let them go ahead of you, or be extra polite when moving past them in an aisle. This can balance out the negativity in their lives. Every act can be a friendly acknowledgment that someone sees they exist and shows them respect. When prolific shoplifters are asked why they choose not to steal from some places, the answer is often attention — not a fear of getting caught but guilt to repay friendliness with theft. We can be the reason others are cynical, or have hope for the world.

CHAPTER 6

Community

I saw the old woman, leaning over her porch. When done with a tissue, she let it drop off into the empty corner lot next to her home. I yelled from my car, stopped at a red light. "Don't you have a garbage can?!" She went inside, and I couldn't tell if she felt anger or shame, the latter being my hope. I'm not going to tell you I wouldn't do it again. But did it really make a difference?

I do know I made a difference with my daughter when she was about eleven. We were driving past Lafayette Square in downtown Buffalo. It's not that large – a bit of greenspace and sidewalks with a monument – but is usually pleasant. That day one of us noticed it was littered with trash. I found myself a bit angry about that and suggested we "fix it" by picking it up ourselves. Twenty minutes later, feeling much satisfaction, it looked immaculate.

Was it someone else's job? Was it fair that we didn't make the mess? Does that really matter so much that I should just be annoyed and do nothing? This was one of the inspirational moments that led me to writing this book.

It's also about being imaginative and taking initiative. Bob Kell, a friend of mine in a business networking association, died unexpectedly, leaving behind a 6-year-old daughter, Amanda. I got it into my head to hold a party on my back deck in honor of him and collected money to be turned into a savings bond. It wasn't much, but was given to the mother to give to Amanda when she was to start college. It might only pay for a few books, but the sentiment was to let her know that her dad was loved by those who knew him.

Belonging to social or civic groups provides opportunities to make the world a better place — and in two very different ways. First, there are many organizations that are or have charities for various causes, either raising money or through volunteerism. These days, more personal, one-on-one volunteer work is more common. Meals on Wheels, teaching people to read, installing smoke alarms, and other activities come to mind.

The other way is to make a difference in the lives of other members. Loneliness is the psychosocial pandemic of our time, and yet just doing social activities doesn't seem to help. People are more generally connected – especially with the "ambient intimacy" of the Internet – but still having no one, or almost no one, they would call a true friend. Being in an organization or club or fraternity provides an opportunity to mentor and be mentored. Why not visit older members who can't get out, or those in hospitals and nursing homes? I have visited many people in these circumstances, and many of them I had not even met before! Those little visits may seem casual, but are deep, personal, and not easily forgotten.

It's also easier to get into the swing of visitations and have easier access if you get credentialed as a minister. As an Interfaith minister myself, I have a badge issued from one of the local hospital systems that lets me visit or deliver things outside of regular hours. It also usually doesn't count against visitor limits, so you can meet with family and offer prayers* and assistance.

The bottom line is that there are plenty of groups to affiliate ourselves with, and nearly all of them could use members. Get as little or as much involved as you wish, being considerate of the organization's expectations. Churches could be considered, and some are welcoming to outsiders without insistence to enroll in their particular denomination.

Cultural societies are generally open to those outside their ethnicity. I know this because I involve myself in the local Hellenic Festival put on b y the local Greek Orthodox Church — and I am neither Greek, not Orthodox. I just love the community and have the ability to help.

Find your tribe, no matter how different or diverse they may be.

Be serious if you say you will pray for someone. Keep a list, physcially or digitally, that you can look at from time to time. This also provides a list of people to check in on, something greatly appreciated. (For more guidance on this, consult my book, "50 Shades of Pray")

CHAPTER 7

Random Acts of Kindness

L et's talk about action on a personal level.

Any act of kindness or generosity can make a difference in someone else's life. And you don't have to belong to a group to do such things. It doesn't have to be planned. All you have to do is be open to opportunities to do good deeds. Some call these "random acts of kindness" and people who go out of their way to do them are "RAKtivists".

There are dozens of examples throughout the book. But there's no way to cover every possible situation where you can be kind. You can even go out of your way to tackle little injustices head on. Think it's unfair that children can't receive a meal in school because they're behind on payment? Go to the office and offer to pay off one or more accounts. Someone's garbage can fell over? Right it. (Bonus points if you are getting it out of the way of traffic!)

Randomness doesn't have to be unplanned. It could be random for the person you reach. When there are coupon books sold for charity (such as Wendy's around Halloween, with proceeds going to the Dave Thomas Foundation for adoption), I try to buy a bunch and then and give them to people who appear homeless. Last year, I gave some to my daughter to give to the residents of the group home where she worked. With a little extra money, gift cards may be a good option.

But actual help instead of dollars makes more sense in a world where we are taught "vagrants" just want money for alcohol or drugs. Sometimes, I use a legitimate excuse not to give money but help anyway, saying, "I don't carry cash, but I can grab you something while I'm in the store."

When I can, I try not to make it look like charity. I'll grab something extra at a food stand and then say, "I can't eat all this. Do you want some?" I've also sneaked water bottles (or the coupons mentioned above) into the cart or satchels of people sleeping on the street. This isn't hard to do while out and about, planned or not.

"Thinking of You" cards go a long way, for condolences, wishes to get well, or for no reason at all. They could be anonymous, or you could send a batch to the Veterans in a nursing facility. Instead of cards, you could send toiletries and socks. The opportunities for such simple giving are endless.

Want to go really outside the box? Friends of mine, Bob and Susan Hubbard, started the "Justice League of WNY", one of many cosplay clubs out there, where members dress up as superheroes (a trademarked term, but I really don't care). Their main purpose is to visit and raise money for comic and coloring books and other items to brighten the days of children in hospitals. Superheroes, indeed.

Why not be Santa Claus? Drop off gifts anonymously at shelters or group homes. Why not visit people who are stuck working overnight on Christmas Eve and give them a little package of something with a bow or ribbon? It could be a coffee shop gift card or little trinket. The receiver doesn't even have to celebrate Christmas — it's the thought that counts. "Have a Blessed Holiday Season" is a cover-all in such situations.

You can also offer your company. Waiting for my daughter (who was touring the Sears Tower), I engaged in conversation a laid-off airline pilot who just got a lower-paying job, not making enough to rise above homelessness.

Another time, I had time to kill in Manhattan and there was a homeless man with a sign asking for baby supplies. After grabbing hot dogs for both of us, I spent an hour sitting on the sidewalk with him. It must have been an unusual sight — him in worn fatigues and me in a suit and tie! It was heartening to see people coming up to him with business cards representing services he could use. A few dollars were dropped his way. I eventually grabbed a few things for his newborn from the store behind us and wished him well. It was a unique way of people-watching, for sure, and I got to know the story of another human being sharing this earth. I truly feel like we all win when we humbly connect with each other.

People who are homeless have an even greater need for connection. They are invisible, yet feel exposed. I can't imagine it, though most of us are closer to the possibility of such an existence than we realize. Connecting with someone in that position, even for a moment, reaffirms their humanity — and reminds us how real such a life is, not just a statistic.

But it's not just the underprivileged or down-and-out. Everyone's life could be a little better, a little happier. Consider everyone – family, friends, and strangers – a target for your good deeds.

CHAPTER 8

For the Earth

After ccollege, I ended up working at my father's company in the plastics industry. The company focused on post-industrial recycling — buying scrap and grinding it into "regrind" that could be put back into machines to make products. I opened up the market to buy and sell post-consumer material, and helped keep over a million pounds of milk jugs and detergent bottles out of landfills.

The plastics industry has a bad wrap. Much of our waste is now this ubiquitous material. I was always the "someday I want to join Greenpeace" sort of guy, so I wanted to know the pros and cons of the industry. I found out that it was a constant improvement, with it being more and more cost-effective to recycle, and less polluting in the life cycle of products and their transportation than other materials. But this isn't about defending my job or industry. No matter what materials we use, it's really population and consumption that skyrocketed.

I started reading "The ULS Report" (paper version back in those days), and I learned the three Rs — Reduce, Reuse, Recycle. It suggested myriad ways to curb pollution and the waste stream by everyday choices. In our house, the most common reuse is plastic grocery bags. We've converted mostly to canvas totes, but whatever bags we get become liners for our smaller trash cans in the house.

I know what some are thinking. If other countries or companies are responsible for most of our pollution or environmental degradation, buying a more efficient vehicle and returning bottles and cans doesn't matter. DO IT ANYWAY. It's not some social experiment to control the masses. Even if it might not save us in the end, it's personal power. It's defiance against those who don't care. Freedom is deliberately exercising the choices we have, and we have plenty.

My daughter tried to start a trend as a student at SUNY Fredonia to get people to drink beverages without straws and lids. I think the marketing slogan was (or should have been) "Don't suck; go topless". To this day, I don't use a straw or lid unless it's for the car. The little savings of material, times the number of times, times the number of people, along with so many other little things people choose to do, can (re)move mountains.

Consuming more, according to the "Broken Window Fallacy", gives people work and churns the economy. When the economy is bad and businesses are hurting, I try to spend a little more money. Any other time, I reuse and hand down (donate) whatever I can. I give old things a new life. Less materials need to be extracted or fuel used. If we don't rush to make more and more, it will be more likely there will be enough for future generations.

My wife's family passed down a saying from the Great Depression that fits in nicely here.

Use it up;
Wear it out;
Make it do,
Or do without.

Take energy efficiency seriously. You can save a fortune by watching consumption and getting better appliances, windows, insulation, LED bulbs, etc.. This seems purely self-serving, but then why it is encouraged by municipalities? It's not just to stop some environmentalists from crying. It means more reliable access to energy in times of greater demand. It means not straining the grid. And in the end, it can mean cleaner water and air. I remember breathing in the 1970s, and have nearly forgotten the smell of diesel and other fuels lingering about. Omissions have improved that much.

But it's also our habits. Carpooling benefits are environmental, economic, and social. Grouping errands saves time as well. How much impact can a shift in behavior have across a community? When people started working mostly from home during the COVID-19 pandemic, the citizens of Los Angeles experienced a smog-free city for the first time in decades. The two days after the 9-11 attacks in 2001 showed a half-degree Fahrenheit rise in temperature, simply because of the lack of global dimming caused by air traffic contrails. I won't debate her about anthropocentric global warming, or if the sky is falling, or the ice age coming. But we KNOW our choices as people, citizens, countries, and a species affect the condition of our world, not just over time, but right now.

Agricultural sustainability is vital if we want to all eat, but what can we do personally? Plant a kitchen garden, place potted herbs in the window, use landscaping that encourages pollinators. Decide the cost in time and effort you are willing to devote. We can even give our excess produce to a neighbor or soup kitchen. We can compost and put out fewer bags on the curb. Sometimes we even have a pet, such as a guinea pig or rabbit, to help us with scraps of greens. Some foodstuffs, including bones, can be used to make broth and other items. Why waste anything? Old-fashioned ways can preserve a lot of, well, preserves. Extra produce can be canned. Some canned goods even make great personal gifts.

Donating to thrift stores is good, but Groups like Freecycle and Craigslist can also be a boon for people who need items and are willing to take used ones that would otherwise be discarded. Always think of giving away first. In some places, you can even leave broken items and construction materials on the curb and it will be gone before the garbage man comes. Metal scrappers are particularly diligent in taking away things made of or containing metal.

When it comes to having a lifestyle that is more about the long game than immediate results, some people ask, "What is the point?" That is what the next chapter is about.

CHAPTER 9

For the Future

According to rugby player Nelson Henderson, "The true meaning of life is to plant trees, under whose shade you do not expect to sit." But planting trees isn't the only thing that endures. And I don't just mean the consequences of our actions causing a ripple effect. Being an organ donor can be life-giving and life-changing when you no longer need your body. (Donating blood and being a live donor is no small thing either!) But did you know you can donate your voice?

On Librivox, you can volunteer your reading skills and help create an audiobook of a work in the public domain. You can also participate in voice banking, such as VocalID, which will turn clips of your speaking voice, mixed with that of others, into a natural digital voice used by those who cannot speak. You can even make personal recordings, audio or video, and read books or give advice to grandchildren you may never meet. If made public, you could be a virtual grandparent of sorts for some distant child long into the future.

What about a book? You could write it yourself or have someone help you. It could be your memoirs, or poetry, or a how-to book for one of your hobbies. Ot you may prefer making videos or podcasting. It doesn't matter how few people come across it, so much as it is

EVERYDAY JUSTICE – 31

out there. You never know who you might inspire someday, in a way that only you as a person could uniquely do.

Willing part of your estate to charities may be an option. You might set up a scholarship fund or trust for some other purpose that benefits the community or mankind. You could have messages planned to be given after your death as a meaningful goodbye. Imagine all the possibilities.

In the end, our greatest legacy will be those who follow in our footsteps, family or otherwise. A friend posted a saying on social media today (attribution unclear) that sums it up nicely: "I want to leave a legacy that can be heard in the way my children speak to strangers."

This all assumes you care about what happens when you're gone. You may not feel as invested if you don't have children, but we're all sharing this existence nonetheless, and that ought to mean something. Heck, if you believe in reincarnation, you will inherit the earth you helped make the way it is, for better or worse!

CHAPTER 10

Be The Light

"It's better to light a candle than to curse the darkness" is the theme of this book. But it's more than that. I've always said that it is untrue that life isn't fair. It is *people* who are unfair. And we can choose not to participate in that. Over time, we can create a community of like-minded individuals, building a circle of trust and integrity among friends and acquaintances.

This reminds me of another saying, "If there's no light, be the light."

Father James Keller, founder of the Christophers in New York City, writes, "Thousands of candles can be lighted from a single candle, and the life of the candle will not be shortened. Happiness never decreases by being shared." Bad moods are contagious, but so are smiles. Ignorance can spread, but so can civility. And when we play the positive side of things enough, people look up to us. They may even get upset when we fail, expecting us to be perfect. But even that is a testament that you bring light more often than not.

Ram Dass once said that even in the depths of hell, all you must do is offer the question, "What needs to be loved?" When you make a habit of living this way, the world around you changes, your perception of it, and the perceptions of others.

Let's consider the relationship between love and charity. There is a word in a letter of Paul of Tarsus that is variably translated as "Charity" and "Love". We may read about Faith, Hope, and Charity, and that the greatest of these is Charity. But the version with the word Love is more commonly found at weddings (and on shirts, pillows, and mugs), for obvious reasons. Why two very different translations? Perhaps the confusion is that "charity" comes from the Latin "Caritas". But it doesn't mean charity in the usual, modern sense. Centuries ago, the term was closer to "affections people ought to feel for one another" rather than acts of kindness. Today, we usually think of alms-giving and not much else.

The original word used was the Greek word ἀγάπη (agape), meaning Love. But as there were so many words for love in Greek, let's be specific. Agape is pure, unconditional, altruistic Love. It could even be considered Divine. This tells me that true Charity is really an act of loving kindness. Yes, you can make a difference by donating clothes or food items, but what about intention? Making room in your closet or getting rid of an overstock of Lima beans isn't an act of love. It's like the difference between a diet to lose weight with fasting as a spiritual discipline.

Taking a small, personal action, then another, then another, builds a sincere attitude of "caritas". Instead of just seeing the bright side of choices that help others, we start to look for them. Charity and kindness become a habit — and a meaningful way of life that can't help to set the world a bit more right.

True charity isn't for praise or as a social media photo op. There is something to be said for anonymity, or selectively letting only certain people know, for practical reasons or to involve them in the deed. Sometimes you WANT others to know there is good being done in the world, with or without your name on it, especially if it is an example others can easily follow. A mega-donation won't usually spur on others to donate to a charity, but selling candy bars or asking for donations on your Facebook birthday fundraiser might. Cleaning up after yourself may set the standard others might follow. Normalize good deeds of all kinds, especially the random helping of strangers.

You can also help others be a Light just by doing this one, often difficult thing — asking for help. Give others a chance to do something. We feel empowered by helping others, and by not needing help, but the latter throws away an opportunity. An old Zen saying tells us, "The giver should be thankful." We are blessed by the works we do for others. It builds gratitude, and makes us better people. Let others have that experience. It can even turn an adversary into a friend, or at least an ally. I have found this to be true, as have others I know.

I will end this thought with a quote from J.R.R. Tolkien:

> Some believe it is only great power that can hold evil in check, but that is not what I have found. It is the small everyday deeds of ordinary folk that keep the darkness at bay. Small acts of kindness and love.

The world will go on with or without you, but it won't be the same. There is so much wrong in the world, but you can defy the injustice of it all. You can go against the flow of bad things and behaviors of others by not participating in it. You can set this or that right, here and now, set an example, and shift the balance of life in everyone's favor so long as you choose to do so.

-

Afterword: A Wonderful Life

At the beginning of this book, I talked about my own challenges —my anger and despair over the injustices in the world. And let me be clear, with no bragging intended: I practice what I preach here. But does it help?

Sometimes. It still feels like the world is coming apart at the seams. There are still people who do things that are impolite, inconsiderate, ignorant, unfair, or hateful. There are even things I catch myself being guilty of. Being informed doesn't help. Conflicts over human and civil rights are closing in on our communities in places and ways we never thought it could happen. We can't even agree on what is and is not genocide, or who deserves rights. The powerful fund lies, hatred, death, and attack anyone who speaks out or brings relief to their victims.

There are times I found it nearly impossible to clear my head in the middle of writing this book. Then, in between foreboding and apocalyptic news snippets, I see stories of people who do amazing, everyday things — gestures of goodwill, sportsmanship, rescue, rehabilitation, reunion, Love, and innocence.

Just now I saw a video about a dog with one of their legs cut off. They were taken in by a loving family, cared for, and proved conclusively to me that dogs can smile. I look to my left and see Hazel Nut Butter napping on a beanbag in my office. A pit-mix, she was removed from her previous owner as a puppy and was very ill. My wife, working for a veterinarian at the time, assisted the SPCA in caring for her. Like many other pets over the years, we decided to ensure her a good life. My wife jokes that she's a "lemon" in terms of health.

It is hard sometimes to pay off some of the bills. She has to be fed sitting up twice a day and take medication on a schedule, making our own plans a bit challenging. But we provide her a home and all that entails, and she brings us joy. Caring for her is not a burden, but a blessing.

I sometimes hold her in my arms, thinking of all the other animals we have not, or could not, save. I remember that we made a difference for HER, and that is worth something. Even if I can't see or measure the results, I know I made a difference. Because I picked up trash, put a stray cart back, wore a mask when I was sick, or didn't creep up on the crosswalk with my car, or just smiled when I didn't feel like it, I made the world a little cleaner, healthier, safer, happier. Someone's day was made a little better, or someone's life may have been saved.

The opposite of resentment is GRATITUDE. At end of day, try not to dwell on problems out of your reach to fix. Be grateful for what you did do. Like Samwise says to Frodo in Peter Jackson's rendering of The Lord of the Rings: The Two Towers, "There's some good in this world ... and it's worth fighting for." Be grateful you can Fight the Good Fight, and choose to do so. The race is never finished, and you can't always stay on your feet, but the world is always better than it would be if you weren't in it.

APPENDIX: A PRIMER ON VOLUNTEERING

{This document was created by the author in 2014 for use in his Earth2Mouth program and has been shared by others over the years.}

VOLUNTEER PRIMER

Serving those with needs is an act of Mercy that benefits the giver as well as those who receive. All should be thankful for their part in doing something in the spirit of human kindness. But the average person, especially those young and inexperienced with charity projects, may not know what to expect, how to act, and how to deal with problem that may arise.

I'm writing this not as a pep talk or theoretical essay, but simple advice on how to deal what you will experience when you deal with the needy and poor. This advice is written as useful guidelines for the Earth 2 Mouth program in particular, but can be applied to any community service that deals directly with other human beings.

Dress for the Job

Unless there's a specific reason or request to dress up, don't. This doesn't mean to dress unkempt or look like you shouldn't be handling food. Clothes you can work in for whatever tasks you may have to perform is the general rule, remembering there is almost always something to clean up and you may be asked to do it. Clothes can be washed, but you don't want to wear what will make you concerned about being ruined.

For the farm, the weather can change and is not necessarily the same as where you live. Long pants and sleeves might be comfortable for kneeling or protecting from sun, but many wear short sleeves and t-shirts, which is fine (just have and wear sunscreen as necessary). A large-brimmed hat is helpful, gardening gloves are optional, boots might be best if it's muddy and you don't like mud. A light jacket is helpful if it gets chilly or rains.

Jewelry is not an generally an issue, so long as it doesn't interfere with the work at hand. In a proper volunteer environment, there should be no concern about losing valuables. Also, try to avoid controversial messages or images on clothing. Use common sense. Wearing a rival team logo may get a reaction from some, but will not generally cause an unpleasant discussion as would a political slogan for or against some issue or politician.

Talk to Strangers ... Sort Of

The rule "Don't talk to strangers" is good advice for children out by themselves without supervision. With supervision, children do not need to be afraid of the people they are serving. However, this does not mean we dispose of common sense. Personal information should not be shared, and if name tags are used, a first name or nickname should suffice. If asked a lot of questions, the child must know they can simply tell the person they have to get back to work and then do so.

If they are uncomfortable for any reason, they should know they can approach a parent or other chaperone, even if they think it might be "silly" or "no big deal". We in turn must not judge them, and even if it's not an issue that needs action, acknowledge their concern and support their decision to bring it to your attention.

Hunger is Apolitical; Judgments Don't Fit On a Plate

There are plenty of reasons people are in need, and it is all too easy to make assumptions without walking in their shoes. Neither blaming the person or society or the government will address their immediate need, which is the only reason you are there.

In a food pantry, you will see people of every color, gender, age, and appearance. Some of the poor (and even homeless) try to dress as nicely as possible -- even in a suit. Assumptions should not be made based on how much gold is around their neck or if they have a really nice cell phone. Whether someone "needs" our help is not for us to decide. They are asking for it by being there and that should be enough, and not discourage us from helping all those truly in need. Besides, we may have it all wrong as to who is who.

Reach Out, Not Down.

The needy are our equals. We could be among them. At some time in our lives we may have been. And when someone is needy, they don't want to made to feel that way any more than they already do. The point here is not to dwell on circumstance, or treat them differently then you would treat a friend or someone living next door.

Some needy will say or do things that make them seem ungrateful or entitled. What is not seen is that complaining or demanding some little thing like a different dessert is one of the few ways they can exert control over something in their lives. If they take a full serving and don't finish it, that's alright, even if wasted food makes us cringe. They are not children or animals, and their right to not eat everything in front of them is a way of not giving in to dire circumstances dictating such a basic thing as what they eat.

One approach is to consider them customers you want to make happy, not broken people to be fixed. They want to be treated like anyone else, and doing so is the best way to show simple human respect they may not get elsewhere.

There will usually be some children. This may really touch volunteers, especially if they are children themselves. That's okay. Just don't show it outwardly. Too much concern or reaching out can be taken as condescending or make the people – who are more than aware of their circumstances – uncomfortable or even upset.

Scary Is Relative

Extreme circumstances are few and far between, and places that serve the general public are prepared to deal with them. The most common problem is someone becoming belligerent or having a mental or physical health issue.

If someone needs help (or attention) of any sort, the official staff of the location should be made aware of it and THEY should handle it. It is common they would know the individual having a problem, such as someone appearing drunk having a history of diabetic reactions. Some people may have been banned from the premises, or want special treatment because they "know" someone in charge. Never assume anyone has permission to do or receive something against the rules and common sense. Again, go to whoever is in charge and make it clear it is not your decision to make.

Some people talk (and mumble) to themselves, a lot. By itself, this is not a problem or any warning sign. It may be due to a person's mental condition, but is often a means to be left alone, discouraging others from talking to them. If you ask someone a question and they don't answer you, repeating yourself or trying gently getting their attention is fine, but don't push.

In general, do not make physical contact. A hand on the shoulder if someone is crying over their plate isn't a crime, but there are many reasons some people do not want to be touched at all. Use your intuition and best judgment. This doesn't mean you have to run away from a "little old lady" who tries to give you a hug, but it's your choice, too. This is about safety and respect -- for you and for them. It's rare, but any unwanted contact should be reported immediately.

APPENDIX: FOOD DONATION SUGGESTIONS

{This list, attribution unknown, is a very general guide. Make sure the foods can be accepted by the place you intend to donate them. Many places have restrictions on anything perishable, or without nutritional information, or certain packaging. Some places have school backpack programs for children of households that are food-insecure. Reach out to your local school systems or similar community programs for guidance on what they need.}

1. Everyone donates Kraft Mac & Cheese in the box. But it needs milk & butter which is hard to get from food banks.
2. Boxed milk is a treasure. Kids need it for cereal, which they get a lot of.
3. Everyone donates pasta sauce & spaghetti noodles.
4. Canned foods should be pop-tops OR donate can openers.
5. Oil is a luxury needed for Rice-a-Roni which they get a lot of.
6. Spices, salt & pepper are a real gift.
7. Tea bags & coffee are caring gifts.
8. Sugar & Flour are treats.

9. Fresh produce donated by farmers & grocery stores are important.

10. Seeds are great in spring & summer because growing can be easy for some.

11. Rarely is there fresh meat.

12. Tuna & Crackers make a good lunch.

13. Hamburger Helper goes nowhere without ground beef.

14. They get lots of peanut butter and jelly but NEED sandwich bread.

15. Butter or margarine are good.

16. Eggs are a commodity!

17. Cake mix & frosting make it possible to make a child's birthday cake.

18. Dish-washing detergent is very expensive & is always appreciated.

19. Feminine hygiene products are a luxury & women will cry over them.

20. Everyone loves Stove Top Stuffing.

Author's note: If you work at a food establishment, there may be an additional opportunity. When I worked as a pizza delivery driver, I found out they were throwing out the ends of rolls that were cut off for people buying small subs. It amounted to almost a garbage bag worth of bread some nights, so I started taking it to a food pantry. After doing this a while, they decided if it was good enough to donate, they could cut them differently so there was no "waste". I recommend working something out with the owner or operator, getting them on board. Besides, they probably know of any health codes or policies that may restrict such donations.

EARTH 2 MOUTH PROGRAM

Many years ago, I wanted to teach suburban kids in religious education classes that "Feeding the Hungry" was more than tossing canned goods into a box. Taking them to the St. Vincent de Paul Dining Room, they met the needy face-to-face and it changed them. More recently, Stew Ritchie of Native Offerings, a community-supported agriculture (CSA) farm in East Otto, NY, shared with me his vision of reconnecting people with their food source — instead of seeing it as coming from a can in a store. "Earth 2 Mouth" is a combining of these two ideas, bringing a deep awareness of the real effort and benefit to feeding the hungry.

In a nutshell, it's a community service concept I created that connects local food producers and soup kitchens in an end-to-end volunteer experience.

HOW IT WORKS

Many local farms are short on labor. In exchange for 3-5 hours of work by a group of volunteers, farms give volunteers produce, which then can be written off on taxes as a donation to the food pantry or soup kitchen. Students and citizens alike are looking for volunteer opportunities, including those looking to fulfill service hours requirements. They get the experience of working in the fresh air on a farm and helping their neighbors where the need is greatest. Places that prepare and serve the poor are always in need of food and volunteers. This is the hands-on fulfillment of the days work, where people can actually serve others wholesome, fresh food they may have picked themselves.

The challenge is planning. We piloted the program with volunteers from the Unitarian Universalist Church of Amherst, coordinated by then-Seminarian Michelle George. We all worked at Native Offerings Farm, bringing and preparing the bounty to the clients of Friends of Night People in Allentown (a neighborhood on Buffalo's West Side). We rarely ran the program since due to constraints on the people involved.

Ideally, someone could establish a database of participating farms, volunteer groups, and places which serve food to the poor. Nothing would please me more than for others to steal this idea and make it work in diverse communities.

PRESENTATION VIDEO

{The detailed explanation below is a transcript of a video based on a speech I gave to an ecumenical group back in 2011. It's currently available on YouTube.}

My name is Ken Stuczynski ... and I eat food.

My story is probably the same as many of you here. When I was little, food appeared on my plate three times a day. It came from a can or box or bag from the kitchen cupboards. It was only when I was older did I realize where food really comes from.

The supermarket. So it was of no surprise to me that if we wanted to give to the poor, you simply put a can IN a bag or a box. Lima beans, right? Like the supermarket represented some magical place where food comes from, that box represented the mythical race known as the Needy.

I grew up in the suburbs. I lived in a comfort zone where food appeared and disappeared, and none of it was of consequence to me or the people around me. As I got older, part of me knew this wasn't quite right. So I made the first of two choices in my life I will never regret.

The first choice was in my 20s, as a religious education teacher at Sts. Peter & Paul in Depew. I decided to take my Confirmation students (high school sophomores and juniors) to the St. Vincent de Paul Dining Room on Main Street in Buffalo. Strangely, nothing like this had been done before in the parish. Some of these kids had never even been in the city, a mere six miles away.

And one of my students – a class clown, but not a bad kid – was silent the whole way back. Afterward he said, very seriously, almost in tears, "I didn't expect to see children." Maybe it's because we never had "children-size" donation boxes in the vestibule...

The point is that for these kids, hunger was never again defined by a television commercial, or a fundraiser for people thousands of miles away they'd never meet. They saw beyond the box to be face-to-face with real people, human beings just like them.

The second decision was a more personal one. In 2002, times were tough. I was a new business owner, and after 9-11, companies stopped spending money overall. We lived within our means, but a few more food dollars could have went a long way. My wife and I applied for food stamps, and then withdrew our application after we realized that would require us to accept all sorts of other programs we didn't need and even counseling for things that didn't apply to us. It was all or nothing dependency, and we chose nothing.

What I did do is connect with a farm I found out about through one of my Tai Chi students – something I taught evenings for a number of years and now work with Veterans at the Recovery Center in Buffalo. Buffalo Organics, now known as Native Offerings Farm, was a family-owned, community supported agriculture project, or "CSA". This means you purchase a "food subscription" from their harvest, picking up a weekly "share" over during most of the year.

We chose the option of me working on the farm one day a week in exchange for our share, which more than fed us. I needed the exercise and couldn't afford a gym, and we talked about having a farm of our own someday – I may as well know for sure if I'd enjoy the work and lifestyle ahead of time. So here I was, doing all that in the fresh air, AND bringing home more food than my wife could freeze and can for the winter.

A CSA is a business model, for sure, but is founded in a philosophy that I learned from Stew Ritchie, the father of the family who owns the farm: People need to be connected to their food source. He wanted people to KNOW where their food comes from. It isn't something that appears magically from a replicator on Star Trek or the other side of a counter at a restaurant. It was touched and nurtured by Mother Nature – and human hands.

A Step Backward to Go Forwards

And it reminded me of how little we are connected to what is real – the Earth itself, and our fellow Man. Maybe it's because our society is so comparatively prosperous and technologically advanced – and our bureaucratic tendencies are epic in proportion to actual benefits. The result has been that we live almost entirely a life of abstraction. We are sheltered – or shelter ourselves rather – from the reality of both our natural environment and human needs.

In simpler times, there were simpler solutions.

In my grandparent's living room years ago – and now in my own – are a pair of paintings. The Angelus depicts field workers pausing for prayer during the work day.

The Gleaners tells the reality of the artist's time, and many centuries before that. Poor women and children had the right to glean the fields for whatever leftover crops they could gather for themselves, after the harvest. Jean-François Millet painted these in the late 1850s, long before the birth of anyone now living.

In September 2010 and again in July 2011, we did exactly that.

In exchange for the labors of a few volunteers for a few hours, we filled our cars with fresh organic produce, some of which would have been left in the fields unharvested. The farmer – the Ritchies in this case – got a few extra chores done and can claim a donation on their taxes. We brought it to the Friends of Night People, where we prepared what we could integrate into the evening meal, and stored the rest for their future use.

Both nights we served between one and two hundred men, women, and children. There were no lima beans. There was no box. It was food worthy of the effort and dignity of human beings. It was a long day of work, and there were no complaints, only satisfaction, and smiles.

The Bigger Picture

In countries where hunger is a much more serious problem, we have ignored the fact that generations of aid from wealthier countries have not changed the fundamental conditions of hunger. Food is not being grown where it can be, not getting to the people who need it, and is even used as a weapon of war and genocide. At best, it's a tax write-off and anti-guilt pill for the haves, a precarious hope of survival for the have-nots.

What is turning the tide – virtually eliminating widespread hunger, community by community in places around the world – are programs that do not just give out food, but secure an infrastructure that feeds people even in yearly droughts and disrupted governments. LOCAL food banks. Local supply requirements for school food programs. Guaranteed markets for small farmers.

So what we are trying to do here is of no less consequence than global actions. Geographic distance is irrelevant. Scale is irrelevant. What we have the opportunity to do here is what can simply be done, and it is enough to bring awareness and change to the relationship in our own community between the earth, food, and the hungry.

The Program

The action plan is simple – volunteers work with local farmers in exchange for food that can then be served to the needy.

The strategy is simple – establish relationships with farmers, soup kitchens, and groups of volunteers, such as churches or schools where students are looking for community service hours.

The model is simple – no one "owns" the program, and it can be borrowed and replicated by anyone, anywhere, with groups of people coordinated through anyone willing to do the work.

The politics are simple – this is a fully volunteer-oriented process, and no money exchanges hands, with people pitching in with transportation costs as they see fit. No budget, no monetary disbursements, no taxpayer money or corporate obligations.

What are left are challenges.

I stand here today in front of you a single person with a few contacts and committed volunteers. The program has been successfully piloted, the plan made public, and a social media presence that I am willing to devote my own professional resources to.

What is needed the most are people who have contacts or are willing to make contacts to fill in a database of farms, kitchens, and volunteer groups and individuals. In particular, we are having trouble finding places that serve the needy late enough in the day to glean and transport produce beforehand.

We could do it on separate days or simply drop off food at a pantry for later use. However, that is not the full the point of the program. The primary purpose is to create an end-to-end volunteer experience that puts us in deeply touch with the reality of need. This is an Act of Mercy, not the difference-at-a-distance that breeds complacency of conscience.

The intention is to transform those making the sacrifice of time and effort, forever changed as more compassionate human beings. Donations and volunteering are things of the moment. We are looking for a new way to approach hunger and thus a sustained spiritual change in ourselves.

There are many programs that do the former, which is by no means unimportant. But the integrity of this program depends on the broader view – working as an integrated local community rather than the usual shifting dollars and hours.

The way I see it, there is no excuse for hunger, not where we live, and not in the bigger world. The only thing left is to decide if we're going to take responsibility as individuals and a community, and this, I pray will be an immediate yet long-term solutions.

ABOUT THE AUTHOR

Ken JP Stuczynski is an Interfaith minister with lifelong interests in everything from world cultures and history to psycho-social phenomena.

His degree is in Philosophy with a concentration in Ethics and a minor in Psychology. He has written articles and essays on the topics of science and religion, society and politics, business and economics, technology and futurism. Using interdisciplinary contexts, many of these focus on the ideals of intellectual honesty and tolerance. Ken is also a Masonic author and speaker, giving presentations and writing articles that have been republished around the world.

The founder of Amorphous Publishing Guild, he lives in South Buffalo with his wife and pets, where he runs his longstanding web development business, Kentropolis Internet. In addition to various community service projects, he enjoys martial arts, carpentry, and keeps bees from time to time.

To learn more about Ken and get on his mailing list, visit
KenVille.Net

ALSO BY THE AUTHOR

50 Shades of Pray
Some White Guy's Book
And Then They Were Gone ...

COMING SOON

Knightly Stewardship: Chivalry in a Modern World

ABOUT AMORPHOUS

AmorphousPublishingGuild

Amorphous Publishing Guild is an exclusive, private publishing company that supports independent writers who want to learn and grow together as published authors. There is no limitation on subject or genre, but only the quality of prose, poetry, and purpose.

Our authors have both on-demand printing and distribution availability to nearly 40,000 outlets, including Amazon, Barnes & Noble, independent booksellers, universities, and libraries. A variety of back-end author services ensure a professional result without the usual limitationsself-publishing .

We can be contacted at *tophat@amorphous.press*.

www.Amorphous.Press

www.ingramcontent.com/pod-product-compliance
Lightning Source LLC
Chambersburg PA
CBHW070031030426
42335CB00017B/2377